The Big Question™

Does the world need more servant-leaders?

Published by Adventurous Publishing
Copyright © 2024 Vince Pizzoni

All Rights Reserved. No part of this publication may be reproduced, stored in a retrieval system, or transmitted in any form or by any means without the prior consent of the author. This includes any form of binding or cover other than that which it is published, and similar conditions must be imposed on subsequent purchasers.

Paperback ISBN:
Hardback ISBN:

Welcome to this edition on

Leadership

Ft Vince Pizzoni

Contents

Our Why

Introduction

Chapter *one* - *Origins*

Chapter *two* - *Finding purpose*

Chapter *three* - *Authenticity*

Chapter *four* - *The art of storytelling*

About the author

Notes

The Big Question - *'Our why'*

The Big Question is a brand that delve's deep into the minds of influential leaders and uncover their strategies through asking Big questions.

We believe that the journey from aspiration to achievement is both fascinating and instructive.

By asking leaders profound questions about their experiences, we gain valuable insights that can guide you in turning your own dreams into tangible outcomes.

THE B!G QUESTION.

Welcome to this edition in The Big Question book series on Originality.

In this book we speak to Vince Pizzoni, on leadership and selfless-ness.

Introduction

Beginnings

Leadership is a word that gets thrown around a lot. We hear it in corporate boardrooms, motivational speeches, and even in everyday conversations. But as I've navigated my own career and worked with countless leaders across industries, I've realized something that's often missing from these discussions: the true essence of leadership isn't about power, prestige, or control. It's about service.

Far too often, leaders make critical mistakes—mistakes that don't stem from a lack of knowledge or experience, but from a failure to understand what leadership should be about. Many leaders operate from a place of self-interest, prioritizing their own goals over the needs of their teams.

They view leadership as a means to achieve personal success, rather than as an opportunity to empower others. This approach leads to disengaged teams, poor decision-making, and, ultimately, failure.
I've seen it happen time and again: leaders who focus more on their status, on maintaining control, or on looking good to their superiors, rather than doing what's right for their teams.

They micromanage, make decisions in isolation, and neglect the importance of empathy. These are the leaders who fear failure more than they value growth, who care more about their reputation than the well-being of those they're supposed to lead. And the results? Low morale, lack of innovation, and teams that feel undervalued and overworked.

In a world that often glorifies power and control, we need more leaders who are willing to serve. Leaders who understand that true success isn't measured by how much they achieve personally, but by how much they enable others to achieve.

As I reflect on my own journey, I've come to see that servant leadership isn't just the right way to lead—it's the only way to create lasting impact.

Chapter one

Origins

I was born into a family of Italian immigrants who settled in the UK with nothing but the clothes on their backs and a fierce determination to give their children a better life. My father, a prisoner of war, and my mother, who grew up during the same troubled period, didn't have the privilege of education.

They left school at eleven years-young to work and help their families survive. They were the hardest-working people I've ever known, yet they lived with an unwavering love and belief that their children would do better.

That belief wasn't about pushing us to earn money or achieve status. No, their focus was on the deeper value of life—making the most of the opportunities we had and recognizing the uniqueness in every individual. My mother would always say, "Everyone is special, Vince. Each person has their own unique gifts."

That message stayed with me. I carry it into everything I do now, whether I'm mentoring young people, coaching executives, or sitting on a board.

Chapter two

Finding Purpose

The energy sector was where my professional journey truly began. I remember the summer internship I did at an ExxonMobil oil refinery when I was still at university. Eight weeks of intense learning, and I loved every minute of it.

I didn't get the job with them immediately after graduation—funny how life works like that—but I stayed persistent. Eventually, I found my way back to ExxonMobil, and from there, my career took off.

For 15 years, I traveled the world, managing teams, learning about different cultures, and immersing myself in the global energy landscape. It was thrilling, but as I rose through the ranks, I found myself less interested in the technical aspects and more focused on the people. I began to see leadership not as a position of authority, but as an opportunity to mentor and empower those around me.

In managing large teams, I quickly realized that leadership is not about being the smartest person in the room or having all the answers. It's about enabling others to thrive. When I helped my team succeed, I succeeded. It was as simple as that. And yet, so many leaders I encountered didn't see it that way.

Chapter *three*

Authenticity

One of the biggest problems I've seen in leadership, especially in large corporations, is a culture of fear— fear of failure, fear of taking risks, fear of stepping out of line.

Too many managers play it safe, keeping their heads down because they're afraid that if they make waves, their career will suffer. But here's the irony: when you play it safe, you stagnate. And when the leader stagnates, so does the team.

Another issue I've observed is the phenomenon of the "accidental manager." The Chartered Management Institute conducted a survey not long ago, revealing that 80% of managers in the UK are accidental managers.

They've been promoted into leadership roles not because they're suited for it, but because there was nowhere else for them to go. They get pushed into these positions without training, and they struggle because they lack the skills to lead.

And then, of course, there's a lack of empathy. Poor managers are often those who care more about themselves than they do about their teams. They don't see the value in investing in people, and that's where they fail.

I've always believed in the idea of a servant leader—someone who puts their team first and focuses on their development.

When you care more about your team's success than your own, something amazing happens: you all succeed together.

Chapter *four*

Storytelling

Mentoring has become one of the most rewarding aspects of my life. Whether it's guiding students at universities and business schools like Nottingham, London Business School, Imperial College Business School and Cambridge Judge Business School, or sitting down with senior executives who are navigating complex career decisions, I've come to see how much difference it makes when someone invests in you.

Over the years, I've noticed that many of the people I mentor come from underrepresented backgrounds—women, people of color, those from disadvantaged communities. It's no coincidence. The energy sector, like many industries, has historically been male-dominated, with women making up only about 20% of the workforce. I've made it a personal mission to help change that.

When I mentor someone, it's not about ticking a diversity box. It's about helping them see opportunities they may never have considered. Many young people, especially those from disadvantaged backgrounds, simply don't know what's out there. They've been told by society—or even by their families—that certain careers aren't for them. It's my job to challenge that thinking.

I often work with an organization called My Big Career, which helps students from disadvantaged backgrounds. When I ask a group of boys what they want to be, most say "footballers." When I ask the girls, they often say "hairdressers." Now, there's nothing wrong with being a footballer or a hairdresser, but those responses often come from a place of limited vision.

They simply don't know what else is possible. My goal is to open their minds. I tell them, "You have unique gifts.

Let's figure out what they are, and let's explore careers that match those gifts." There's no greater feeling than seeing someone light up with excitement when they realize there's more out there for them.

In my career, I've managed some very large teams across different countries, and what I've learned is this: the best leaders are servant leaders. They care more about their team's development than their own personal success.

If you're in a leadership role, your first responsibility is to your people. How can you help them grow? How can you empower them to be their best?

It's not about being in the spotlight or seeking recognition for yourself. It's about making sure your team has what they need to succeed, even if it means stepping back and letting them take the lead.

Servant leadership isn't a soft or easy path. It requires humility, patience, and a willingness to put others first. But I've seen firsthand how effective it can be. When you lead by serving, your team is more engaged, more creative, and ultimately more successful.

So, does the world need more servant leaders? Without a doubt, yes.

The challenges we face today—in business, in society, in our personal lives—require leaders who are willing to put others first. Leaders who can see the value in diversity, who understand that true success comes not from personal gain but from lifting others up.

As I close this book, I'll leave you with the question my mother taught me to ask: What makes you special? What are your unique gifts, and how can you use them to serve others?

Because when you discover that, you're not just leading—you're transforming lives.

THE B!G QUESTION.

My big question to you is…

What **makes you different?**

About the author

Professor in Chemical and Environmental Engineering at the University of Nottingham, Vince has mentored 1000s spanning the whole career lifecycle from school to university, executive and board level, and made it his mission in life to inspire and mentor future generations into STEM, Engineering, Tech, and Energy careers. His other pillars around which he has built his portfolio are education, the energy transition and equity, diversity, and inclusion.

Vince has 40+ years of relevant, global business experience incorporating executive management and board positions in blue chip companies including ExxonMobil, Suez, V. Ships, Nalco, and P&G and with a boutique executive search firm, Preng & Associates, that specialises in executive and board recruitment for companies in the energy sector.

Today he manages a diverse portfolio that incorporates career mentor to undergraduates, graduates and alumni at the University of Nottingham, energy sector career mentor to students and alumni at several prestigious UK business schools including London Business School, Imperial, Oxford, Cambridge and Chicago Booth, and holds Trustee and Non-Executive positions on several boards.

He won the prestigious Chairman's Award as global General Manager of the year at Suez for outstanding performance, and recently the Davidson Medal 2024 from the Institute of Chemical Engineers (IChemE) for global leadership in mentoring, the TechWomen100 2024 Award for Gender Balance and the Men as Allies 2024 Award from the Women's Engineering Society.

Vince is a Trustee/Non-Executive Board member and Ambassador for various organisations including Male Allies UK, the Women in Engineering Society, Female Leaders in STEM Subjects, POWERful Women, MyBigCareer, a charity providing career guidance to students from disadvantaged backgrounds and the South Shropshire Multi-Academy Trust.

Vince is also a member of the Progressiya 2024 initiative and mentors top businesswomen from Ukraine, and is also a mentor for the Cajigo group where he inspires women in tech.

He is a Chartered Engineer and Fellow of several organisations including the IChemE, Energy Institute, Women's Engineering Society, and the Chartered Management Institute. He is a Group Partner of Circklo start-up and a member/volunteer of Graduate Mentor, UN Women UK, the Career Development Institute and European Women on Boards.

THE B!G QUESTION.

Be **you**,
be **bold**,
Go **big**.

TBQ

Notes

...............Go big

..............Go big

..............Go big

..............Go big

...............Go big

...............Go big

..............Go big

..............Go big

..............Go big

..............Go big

..............Go big

...............Go big

..............Go big

..............Go big

...............Go big

..............Go big

..............Go big

...............Go big

..............Go big

..............Go big

..............Go big

..............Go big

..............Go big

..............Go big

..............Go big

..............Go big

..............Go big

..............Go big

in The Big Question

 @thebigquestionhq

www.ingramcontent.com/pod-product-compliance
Lightning Source LLC
Chambersburg PA
CBHW071632040426
42452CB00009B/1589